AUSTRALIA'
BIRDS

A male Emu and chicks.

Contents

INTRODUCTION

With around 750 species, the birds of Australia are incredibly varied. They have adapted to great extremes of habitat, ranging from temperate coastal areas to tropical rainforest to arid desert. The key to their success in conquering these extremes lies in their extraordinary versatility. We may think of birds as primarily experts at flight but many are able, in varying degrees, to run, swim, dive and climb as well!

The first European settlers recognised similarities in Australian birds to those from their homelands. It is only relatively recently that biologists have learnt that the various groups of Australian birds are quite unique – major groups such as bowerbirds, honeyeaters, fairy-wrens, currawongs and frogmouths are found in few other areas of the world. Although parrots and cockatoos are found on most continents, it is in Australia that this spectacular group of birds displays its most extraordinary diversity and colour.

The specific types of habitat for Australian birds include mallee, rainforest, sclerophyll forests and woodland, arid saltbush and spinifex plains and wetlands. Birds have, over a period of millions of years, evolved and adapted to survive in these sometimes hostile environments.

Mallee areas are composed of dense, low-growing acacias and eucalypts which have several trunks growing from ground level. Mallee trees once covered approximately 20% of the

Above *In the shadow of the imposing grandeur of Nourlangie Rock in Kakadu National Park, Anbangbang Billabong is a haven for wildlife and waterbirds.*

Left The fascinating Satin Bowerbird is well known for the male's unusual behaviour. He builds a twig bower, decorates the surrounding floor with blue and yellow objects, and performs elaborate dancing displays to attract the female.

country – in Western Australia, New South Wales and South Australia, but large areas have been cleared for agriculture. Now found mostly in the south of the country, mallee areas are home to specialised birds such as the remarkable Malleefowl and the beautiful Major Mitchell's Cockatoo.

The various types of rainforest in Australia occur mainly on the mountain slopes of the Great Dividing Range, which runs down the east coast from Cape York in the north to the southern tip of Tasmania. Australian rainforests contain a huge diversity of plant species, including tree ferns, palms and giant trees, and support about 140 bird species. These include a large number of fruit eaters such as bowerbirds, fruit doves, fig parrots and cassowaries. Among these, the Superb Lyrebird, Rainbow Pitta and Satin Bowerbird are some of Australia's most beautiful birds. Unlike the forests of south-east Australia and Tasmania, rainforest doesn't burn easily as it is mainly evergreen with a wet climate.

Forest habitats also include the hard-leafed or sclerophyll forests and woodlands found over most of Australia, and brigalow, a mixture of acacia trees and low scrub found in Queensland. These areas are favoured by insectivorous and nectar-feeding birds, including many of the 67 Australian honeyeater species.

Inland, the landscape is composed of vast areas of arid saltbush and spinifex plains which grade into woodland. Many of the birds inhabiting these harsh landscapes are nomadic, flying from one waterhole to the next – playing a vital role in dispersing the seeds of indigenous plants. The flightless Emu, Brown Falcon and several parrot species such as the Budgerigar and Little Corella are all found in these inland habitats.

With a coastline of around 36 000km, there is no shortage of coastal habitat for birds. The islands of the Great Barrier Reef Marine Park are home to huge flocks of seabirds including Red-tailed Tropicbirds and Caspian Terns. Permanent wetlands are mostly found in the coastal zone and support over 100 bird species. Fortunately for the myriad waterbirds that depend on lagoons, swamps and marshes, there is now increasing awareness of the value of these areas. Protected wetland areas include Coorong National Park in South Australia, Kakadu National Park in the Northern Territory and the Hattah Lakes region of Victoria.

Unfortunately many bird habitats have been altered by humans and bird populations are decreasing as a result. Forests have been felled, woodlands cleared for agriculture and land has been drastically overgrazed. Wetlands have been drained and even the mighty Murray River is polluted and its flow reduced by crop irrigation. Despite these problems, Australia has excellent national parks and reserves in which we can still admire and learn about our heritage of wild birds.

Right Perched on a native pine tree, this male Major Mitchell's Cockatoo has just finished feeding its three chicks. Populations of this beautiful bird are declining due to clearing of forested areas for agriculture and the poaching of chicks for the avicultural market.

Left *With its distinctive upswept wings, the elegant White-bellied Sea-Eagle is commonly found around Australia's coastline and inland on large river systems. This bird is extremely graceful in flight.*

BIRDS OF PREY

Hawks, eagles and falcons have captured the imagination of people throughout history being revered by the ancient Egyptians and by falconers to this day. Unfortunately in recent history, birds of prey have suffered persecution by humans more than most other birds, so that many populations are now only a fraction of the numbers of 200–300 years ago. Australia retains a great wealth of birds of prey – some are common and even breed in urban environments. Many are found nowhere else, including the widespread Brown Falcon and the majestic Wedge-tailed Eagle.

Until recently the Wedge-tailed Eagle was considered vermin in several parts of Australia and thousands were killed. However, this magnificent eagle is now protected and has recovered to the level that it is now commonly found in many parts of the country.

Particularly attractive to these birds are the parks, gardens and tree-lined streets of Canberra. Eight species currently breed within the city and a visitor may, with luck, see the Brown Goshawk, Whistling Kite, Black-shouldered Kite, Little Eagle, White-bellied Sea-Eagle, Brown Falcon and Nankeen Kestrel all on the same day.

Left *Now protected, populations of Wedge-tailed Eagles are recovering from persecution. These eagles have largely adapted to feeding on introduced rabbits.* Above left *Found almost all over the world, the Osprey is primarily a coastal bird in Australia. The undersides of the powerful toes are covered in small, spiky scales which assist in grasping slippery fish.* Above right *White-bellied Sea-Eagles usually nest in tall eucalypts and less frequently on cliffs or offshore islands. This single chick is about 10 weeks old and will soon fly from the nest.*

Below *A widespread and common bird, the Brown Falcon feeds on a wide range of prey including small mammals and insects, birds, reptiles and carrion, most of which is taken from the ground. This highly vocal bird is frequently seen perching on roadside utility poles, fences and dead branches.* Right *Preying chiefly on small birds and insects, the Australian Hobby hunts on the wing with a fierce and dashing flight. Breeding pairs use other birds' abandoned nests, which they defend fiercely during nesting.*

Above *Primarily a predator of small mammals, the Barn Owl has an almost worldwide distribution. This silent flying owl has a ghostly, all-white appearance as it hunts over open countryside, especially when seen in car headlights at night.*

Left *The largest member of the Barn Owl family, the Masked Owl is a powerful nocturnal hunter found in forest and woodland. The female (shown here) is considerably larger and darker than the male.*

WATERBIRDS

The diversity of Australia's wetlands creates the perfect conditions for a great variety of waterbirds. Many of these birds are specialists which have evolved to exploit specific types of wetland and the range of food available. They are mainly nomadic, flying large distances, often at night, in search of fresh water. Several waterbird species are now protected within the many valuable wetland areas which have been given National Park or World Heritage status.

Long-legged wading birds such as the Black-necked Stork and Brolga wade in shallow swamps or lagoon edges. The Black-necked Stork stabs at fish and crustaceans with its massive bill while the vegetarian Brolga uses its stout bill to dig in the mud for roots and tubers. Many herons and egrets use a 'wait and see' technique: they remain motionless until a frog or small fish ventures closely enough so that they can spear them with their dagger-like bills.

Several species of duck use a dabbling motion with their bills to sieve the water for aquatic insects. Others such as the Musk Duck and grebes dive in deeper water for food and can submerge themselves for at least one minute.

Inland swamps and billabongs are often short-lived, filling with rains infrequently. When it rains, many waterbird species are quick to exploit the perfect conditions and breed in densely packed colonies.

Left *When feeding, the graceful and often confiding White-faced Heron is very much a generalist and opportunist – this species is equally at home hunting mice and insects in paddocks as it is stalking through the shallows, stabbing at small fish or crabs.*

Left *The Black-necked Stork (also known as the Jabiru) primarily inhabits coastal wetlands of Australia's tropical north. This striking bird is most easily seen in Kakadu National Park, striding through the swamps searching for fish, frogs, eels and small turtles.*

Right *The stately Brolga is one of the largest of the cranes. This species is well known for its complex dancing rituals, where several birds prance with wings held half-open, while trumpeting loudly and bowing their heads.*

Following pages *Herons commonly feed in large, mixed flocks – Large Egrets, Intermediate Egrets, Pied Herons and White-necked Herons can be seen here. The various species benefit from feeding together by disturbing prey.*

Below *The Australian Pelican is one of the most instantly recognised of all Australian birds. Frequently occurring in groups, this species is a superb flier, able to soar for hours at a time and often at great heights.* Right *The extraordinary elongated hind-toe of the Comb-crested Jacana allows this delightful bird to walk on floating water weeds, giving rise to the popular name of Lily-trotter. The three or four heavily streaked eggs are laid in a nest composed of grasses and sedges on the surface of the water.*

Above *Although distinctly aquatic, the Dusky Moorhen can run at high speed when necessary. As well as building a nest purely for breeding, this species builds several resting platforms as playgrounds for the chicks.*
Left *The Australian Darter's ability to swim with its body submerged and only its head and neck above the water's surface has given rise to its alternative name: the Snakebird. Darters are frequently spotted perching motionless near fresh water with their wings outstretched to dry.*

Left *The Musk Duck is unique to Australia and common in the southwest and the southeast. This stiff-tailed diving duck is entirely aquatic and finds it difficult to walk on land.*

Right *The Australian Shelduck moults twice a year and is unable to fly for about one month during the second moult. This is when large moulting flocks gather in southern Australia at favoured salt lakes, where they can spot predators at great distances.*

Left *Black Swans are vegetarian, with a diet of various aquatic plants and algae – which they often pull up from the bottom by up-ending. The cygnets are able to swim within a day of hatching, although they also like to catch a ride on a parent's back.*

Left *Unique to Australia, the Cape Barren Goose is a relatively rare species of wildfowl which breeds mainly on islands in Bass Strait and off the southern coasts of South Australia and Western Australia.*

SEABIRDS

Australia has a huge coastline composed of silt-laden estuaries, high, jagged cliffs, sweeping sandy beaches and beautiful offshore islands. If these, plus the oceans and seas, form a bird's normal habitat and food source, it is regarded as a seabird. Although many seabirds such as shearwaters or albatrosses are difficult to see or study, many others such as gulls and terns are far more familiar and offer unlimited exciting opportunities for birdwatching.

Estuaries provide roosting and feeding areas for species including Silver Gulls and Caspian Terns. Sandy beaches are favoured breeding grounds for Little Terns and provide resting areas for many gulls and other tern species. Offshore islands including the coral cays of the Great Barrier Reef contain the perfect breeding habitat for countless seabirds and islands off the southern coast, such as Philip Island in Victoria, come alive at night as squawking groups of Fairy Penguins clamber ashore and head into the dunes to feed their expectant chicks.

These coastal habitats are crucial to the existence of many seabirds and yet they face a bewildering variety of threats, such as development, pollution and ever-increasing disturbance by humans, dogs and four-wheel-drive vehicles. It is vital that coastal habitat areas are protected to ensure that our seabirds have a viable home for the future.

Left and right The Shy Albatross spends long periods soaring over the southern oceans, where it is usually solitary, except when groups gather near abundant food supplies. This species tends to pair for life, breeding in densely packed colonies on remote islands off Tasmania.

Left *Familiar in urban and coastal areas, the ubiquitous Silver Gull nests in large colonies on offshore islands, as well as inland lakes and salt fields.*

Right *The imposing large Pacific Gull has the most robust bill of any gull species. A black band on the white tail together with the 'auk, auk' or 'ow, ow' calls are useful aids in identifying this bird.*

Right *Fairy Penguins are the world's smallest penguins and also the most nocturnal, only coming ashore to their burrows after dark. Their streamlined shapes make them superbly adapted to life at sea.*

Above *The largest of the world's terns, the Caspian Tern prefers to breed on offshore islands, although it can be seen hunting on lakes. Upon sighting its fish prey, this tern plunge-dives headfirst to grasp the fish in its bill before flying off.*

Above *The Red-tailed Tropicbird is one of the most beautiful of all seabirds. When breeding on remote islands, adult tropicbirds indulge in elaborate courtship flights, where pairs swoop and circle the nesting area with undulating tail streamers.*

Above *Australia's smallest tern is the Little Tern which prefers to breed in small, loose flocks on sandy beaches and spits. Many colonies suffer from disturbance during breeding by humans, dogs and four-wheel-drive vehicles.*

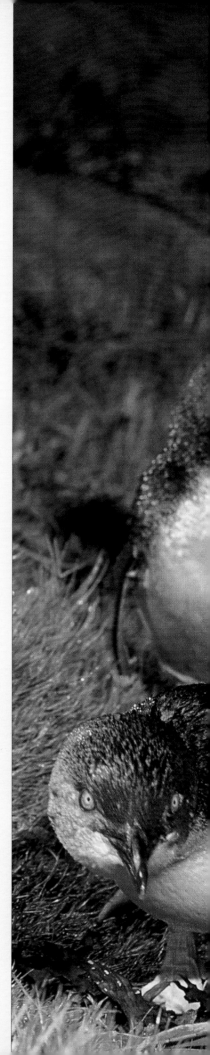

Left *Preferring sandy beaches and estuaries, the Pied Oystercatcher uses its powerful bill to open molluscs such as mussels or to prise small shells from rocks. The striking black-and-white plumage and scarlet bill make this common wader quite unmistakable.*

Above *Often active at night, the Black-fronted Dotterel is a small, vocal wader which inhabits the shorelines of inland lakes, swamps, dams and rivers. Its nest is a scrape in the sand or shingle, where the small pebbles and broken shells help camouflage the eggs.*

Left *A bird of rocky headlands and offshore islands, the Sooty Oystercatcher lays two to three stone-coloured eggs with purple-brown blotches in a depression among rocks, pigface or seaweed.*

BUSH BIRDS AND GROUND BIRDS

The forests, woodlands and scrub areas of Australia are often referred to as 'the bush'. These areas provide suitable habitat for many interesting bird species, including many of the smaller perching birds, or Passerines. Over half of all bird species make up the order known as Passerines, which are distinguished from other birds by the four toes, where three toes point forwards and one points to the rear. These perching birds, as well as birds such as the kookaburra, are not included in the other major bird groups. They are referred to as 'bush birds' in Australia.

Many bush birds build intricate and often beautiful nests in which to lay their eggs and raise their chicks. They include the delicately woven cup of bark, moss and grass of the Eastern Yellow Robin, the domed grass-ball nest of the Superb Fairy-wren and the flask-shaped grass nest of the Zebra Finch. Most of these nests are built in trees or shrubs, so the survival of bush birds is dependent upon a healthy environment and adequate protection of the bush.

Ground birds include some of our most unique and unusual birds such as the flightless Emu (Australia's national bird emblem) and three large-footed mound builders; the Malleefowl, the Australian Brush-turkey and the Orange-footed Scrubfowl. These three fascinating birds are all able to fly.

Left *The Eastern Yellow Robin is a familiar and popular bird of woodlands, forests and gardens. Despite its comon name, this species is a relative of the flycatcher. It feeds on small insects such as spiders, flies and moths.*

Left *Various subspecies of the Australian Magpie, where the back colour varies between black, white and grey, exist in different parts of the country. Often heard at dawn, the magpies' flute-like song is one of the most evocative sounds of the bush.* Following pages *Woodland supports over half of Australia's land birds. Healthy woodland contains an understorey of shrubs with grasses and herbs covering the ground, providing ample food and nest sites for a wide variety of birds.*

Above *The Malleefowl occurs in mallee and scrub areas of southern Australia. This remarkable bird builds a huge mound of sand during autumn. The male visits the mound each day to check and adjust its temperature and when it's ready, the female lays the eggs which are incubated by heat from the sun and fermentation.*

Below *A megapode (or mound builder), the Australian Brush-turkey is found in rainforests and scrub of tropical eastern Australia. This species is common in some suburbs of Brisbane where it can be a nuisance to gardeners.*

Right *European settlement has benefited the Crested Pigeon. This ground feeder eats mainly seed, and is often seen near farms, silos and railway yards where it can become tame.*

Left *Found in a range of wooded habitats throughout Australia, the Common Bronzewing is very much a ground bird. It prefers to walk or run, but it is a wary bird that will burst noisily into flight if disturbed.*

Far left *Found in parties of up to 30 birds, the Rainbow Bee-eater is an attractive summer visitor to much of the mainland. This bird lays its eggs at the end of burrows dug into sandy soil, and several group members help to feed the chicks.*

Left *South-east Australian coastal heathland and woodland with grassy areas form the preferred habitat of the rare Beautiful Firetail. As with most finches, firetails are seed eaters and feed on seeds of grasses, casuarinas and also insects.*

Above *The Zebra Finch is common in many parts of inland Australia, although it is generally found near water-holding areas such as stock tanks and dams. Living in flocks of up to 100, Zebra Finches are highly social birds.*

Right *The male Superb Fairy-wren, with its brilliant blue colouring, is one of Australia's most popular birds. The male is found in family parties, all members of which bring food to the chicks during breeding. Many males revert to a brown plumage during winter.*

Left *The communal Blue-faced Honeyeater is a large honeyeater with a bold and distinctive face pattern. Although they feed on fruit and the nectar of flowering paperbarks and grevilleas, insects make up a large part of their diet.*

Above *Feeding almost exclusively on nectar, groups of New Holland Honeyeaters spend much of the day visiting flowering shrubs such as banksias and grevilleas in the southwest and southeast of Australia. This hopping from blossom to blossom makes them very efficient pollinators.*

Below *The Strong-billed Honeyeater is unique to forests and scrub areas of Tasmania. It feeds in small, conspicuous flocks which noisily tear and probe the branches and trunks of eucalypts and other trees.*

Above and below   *The rollicking, chuckling cacophony of the Laughing Kookaburra is one of the most familiar sounds of the bush. Family groups gather at dawn and dusk with tails cocked and bills pointing towards the skies to chortle their many choruses and advertise their territories to neighbouring groups. Kookaburras are in fact forest kingfishers – possibly the world's largest – which spend much of the day perched on branches looking for prey. Kookaburras live largely on insects, small mammals, lizards, snakes and the occasional small bird.*

Right *After the female Emu lays up to sixteen eggs, the male Emu assumes full responsibility for incubation; once the eggs are hatched, the male looks after the chicks for seven to eight months, after which the chicks start to gain independence.*

PARROTS AND COCKATOOS

Australia may justifiably be called '*Terra Psittacorum*' or 'Land of Parrots'. Virtually no part of the vast landscape of Australia is without parrots. Out of the world's 340 parrot species, approximately one-sixth occur in this country. Visitors are often surprised that such colourful and exotic creatures are so easily observed.

Parrots are distinguished by several features: the colour and brilliance of the plumage, the short, stubby bill and the unusual toe configuration, with two toes pointing forward and two pointing backward.

The humid forests of the eastern coastal regions support many exciting species. Rainbow Lorikeets are frequent visitors to parks and gardens and rosellas and cockatoos can also be seen.

The mallee areas in the south of central Australia are home to a large number of parrot species. The Major Mitchell's Cockatoo breeds in hollows in native pines, while Budgerigars, Purple-crowned Lorikeets and Mallee Ringnecks squabble over hollows in the mallee trees, the Sulphur-crested Cockatoos preferring the ancient red gums that line the river banks.

Throughout Australia, parrots plan their breeding time to coincide with conditions suitable for feeding their young – usually periods of high rainfall.

Left *The brilliant plumage of the Rainbow Lorikeet makes it one of Australia's most popular birds. These fast-flying parrots often visit parks and gardens where their screeching calls and bright colours make them very conspicuous.*

Top right *Found only in Tasmania in a range of habitats from coastal scrub to forests and gardens, the Green Rosella gathers in small flocks to feed on the fruit, seeds and blossoms of native trees and shrubs.*

Bottom right *Purple-crowned Lorikeets are small, swift-flying, noisy parrots which descend in small parties to feed on eucalypt blossom. They often nest in hollows in mallee trees.*

Following pages *This flock of Little Corellas is seen in the Gammon Ranges of South Australia leaving the night roost and flying to daytime feeding grounds.*

Right *Numbering less than 200, the Orange-bellied Parrot is one of Australia's most endangered birds. Breeding only in the south-west wilderness areas of Tasmania, this diminutive parrot crosses Bass Strait to spend winter on the southern coast of the mainland.*

Left *Occurring in large flocks in the wild, the Sulphur-crested Cockatoo is also a popular bird in zoos and aviaries. Screeching parties are often very visible at sunrise and sunset as they fly to and fro between roosting sites and feeding grounds.*
Above *Closely related to rosellas, the Mallee Ringneck is the eastern race of the Port Lincoln Ringneck. These quite large parrots feed in foliage or on the ground, preferring the seeds of indigenous pines, eucalypts, grasses, fruit and the occasional insect.*

Above *A flock of pink and grey Galahs is one of the most evocative sights of rural Australia. Galahs are mainly seed eaters, so have benefited from agriculture. They are seen feeding around railyards and farms or drinking at waterholes.*

Above *Favoured nest sites for Major Mitchell's Cockatoos are hollows of native pine trees (which are formed when high winds break off the tops of trees). This beautiful cockatoo is often seen feeding on the fruit of wild melon plants.*

Above and below *Possibly the world's best known parrot, the nomadic Budgerigar is only seen with a green-and-yellow plumage in the wild. Breeding usually follows periods of rain when noisy groups squabble over nest hollows before laying their four to six white eggs.*